For our mothers,
Nancy and Greta,
for staying young at heart!

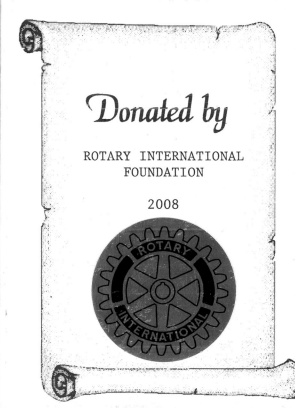

First Edition
Library of Congress
Control Number: 2005910930
ISBN13# 978-0-9708104-4-1 (hardcover)

11 10 09 08 07   10 9 8 7 6 5 4 3

Printed in China

Fairy Houses

... Everywhere!

The traditon of building Fairy Houses

has its roots on several islands off the coast of Maine. For decades families have been inspired to create these whimsical habitats made from pieces of nature for the fairies to visit.

It's easy to feel the presence of fairies in the quiet of the woods when sunbeams float through the ocean mist highlighting the mosses and ferns below.

Surrounded by Nature's beauty—her colors, shapes, textures, sounds and fragrances—one is inspired to create a small habitat using surrounding materials. Twigs, stones, leaves, pine needles and acorn caps become foundations, rafters, roofs, soft floors and dishes.

Perhaps the fairies are hidden in between the layers that Nature reveals to us as we quietly make a gift by leaving a small shelter built with resources at hand.

In these places of splendor it is important to use only natural materials while not harming anything that is still growing.

Discover how fairy houses can be built everywhere, as revealed throughout this magical photographic journey.

Contents

Woodland
Fairy Houses

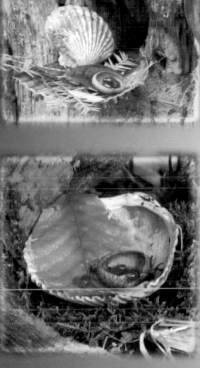

Fairy Boats

Beach
Fairy Houses

Meadow
Fairy Houses

Fairy Houses In Backyard Gardens

Fairies have been sighted in the neighborhood and what better way to entice them to stay than by building them a house! Backyards offer a wealth of materials to use in construction. Cut flowers, seedpods and grass clippings create wonderful colors and textures. Treasures collected from visiting your favorite places—shells, stones and driftwood—add endless possibilities to your fairy house designs.

Keep it simple and rustic, or further your talents by detailing the inside with useful fairy furnishings. Now it's easy to check on your fairy house every day, making home improvements and decorating with seasonal highlights.

24

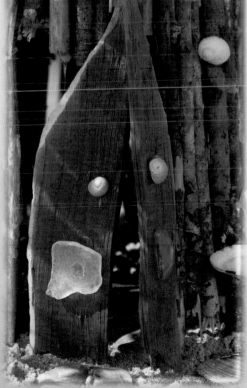

Fairy Houses
In the Air

Fairy House
Mansions

If you don't have a backyard or just prefer an indoor activity there is the "Fairy House Mansion."

Basic materials are still all natural, but with a little hot wax and natural twine you can make a more permanent structure. Using a flat wooden base gives the freedom to move your house to different locations.

These lovely homes can be displayed indoors, or even outdoors when the weather permits. Consider placing it near a window, as it is bound to catch the eye of a passing fairy!

Fairy House
Details

breakfast table

lookout

lounge

outhouse

gazebo

swing

patio furniture

bathroom

boats

43

sauna

garden

picnic table

44

mandolin

dancing ring

tea house

bedroom

Spring

Summer

Autumn

Winter

Fairy Houses ... Behind the Scenes

Visiting an island off the New England coast, we discovered tiny fairy houses in a forest filled with pine trees, ferns and sea mist. The houses were made from twigs, stones, bark and other pieces of nature. Sprinkled along the woodland path, they were tucked under tree roots, around bushes and against rocks.

Fascinated, Tracy scouted out a place to build her own house and became totally absorbed in this enchanting pastime. Her thoughts drifted back to childhood, and out of the blue she felt a twinge of jealousy, realizing no one had introduced this delightful activity to her when she was growing up.

Excited, Tracy had an idea. Why not create a children's picture book that would inspire children and families everywhere to build fairy houses in their own backyards? The idea evolved to become "Fairy Houses," the first book in the award-winning "Fairy Houses Series." It was soon to be followed by "Fairy Boat," "Fairy Flight" and the video "Kristen's Fairy House."

The Series led to many reading and workshop events at libraries, schools, nature centers and botanical gardens where Tracy introduced children to the creative fun of building fairy houses. Attending the events, Barry photographed these delightful fairy houses, some of which are presented in this book.

We listen to children describe their fairy houses in great detail, with pride in their voices and a sparkle in their eyes. Their excitement at nature's frequent visitors—toads, chipmunks and butterflies—is how we came up with the phrase "The Fairy Houses Series connects Kids and Nature... with a pinch of Fairy magic!"

Building fairy houses encourages the child within us all, exploring the imagination and nurturing creativity.

Barry & Tracy Kane

Fairy Houses Garden Tour

Debut of the annual
"Tour of Fairy Houses in Gardens of Portsmouth, NH"

Last September, an innovative neighborhood in Portsmouth, New Hampshire launched "a first of its kind" garden tour. Residents and friends were invited to build fairy houses in their gardens. Their mission was to craft a unique garden experience for all generations to enjoy while raising funds to benefit several non-profits in their area.

Inspired by Tracy Kane's books and her workshops building fairy houses with families, they invited her to become part of the team to make this project a reality. Barry became involved during the planning stages when it was apparent the event was taking fairy house building into new dimensions. He had to photograph the amazing creations this Garden Tour would produce and include them in the book, "Fairy Houses Everywhere," even if it meant delaying its publication.

Participants' ages ranged from 3 to 93—exploring skills from preschoolers to professional architects, with house construction ranging in style from rustic to mansion. The event had all the right ingredients—community involvement, an appeal to all ages, showcasing public and private gardens in all their autumn glory—with the charm of fairy magic. The tour concluded at a park where inspired families created their own fairy houses. It was a fabulous success!

A special thanks to the Friends of the South End Neighborhood Association and the City of Portsmouth for creating a weekend where imagination and enchantment brought smiles to the hearts of everyone, producing delightful pictures and lots of ideas to share.

For more information about the tour, visit www.fairyhouses.com.

Also from Tracy Kane ...

The Magic of Color
by Tracy Kane

"Children's Book Sense" pick
American Booksellers Association

ISBN 0-9766289-0-2
$17.95 US, 40 Pages

Can you imagine an Earth without color?
No blue sky, green grass or brilliant red sunsets?

Two tribes exist peacefully on an island in a world of black and white. A dramatic event occurs creating two colors that transforms their lives. When a third color appears on the mountain peak both tribes set off on an adventure to claim this dazzling new treasure.

Their journey leads them to a startling encounter and they discover a new world more wonderful than any they could imagine.

www.magicofcolor.com